101 AWESOME THINGS

YOU MUST DO IN

LONDON

JAMES HALL

101 AWESOME THINGS YOU MUST DO IN LONDON

For information visit:
http://www.JamesHallTravel.com

ISBN-10: 1543129005
ISBN-13 : 978-1543129007

First Edition: Febuary 2017

10 9 8 7 6 5 4 3 2 1

James Hall

CONTENTS

Foreword

If you're here because you want to visit London, you have come to the right place!

It's not hard to find 101 things to do in London. In fact, you can probably easily find 1001 things to do in London. The difficulty lies in how to choose what to do, and how to pack it all in.

Whether it's a tour on a famous London double decker bus, a trip to watch the Changing of the Guards at Buckingham Palace, or a visit to the gruesome London Dungeon, your time as a visitor to the famous capital will be time well spent.

Whether you're a Japanese tourist or a local "Limey" who's never seen the sights, one thing is for certain: you'll never get bored in London town.

Now you probably heard of the term Limey, but did you have any idea the name was slang for the British navy's sailors because they were given watered down rum mixed with lime juice? The lime juice was to prevent scurvy...They were pretty healthy sailors, at least as far as scurvy was concerned...

In the following pages, go on an armchair adventure while you plan your activities. The aim of this book is to give you the best attractions and activities, so your travels will be enriched and your experiences wonderfully satisfying. The streets may not be paved with gold, but you can make your vacation a fairy-tale that you will treasure and remember forever.

So let's not waste any more time...dive right in!

Chapter 1: Famous Landmarks That You Cannot Miss

You can't go to London and not visit these famous landmarks. You won't be able to hold your head up high if you leave London without going to see Big Ben and Trafalgar Square, for instance.

Your story, when you get back home, just won't be complete if you didn't watch the Changing of the Guard at Buckingham Palace, wander around St James's park or take a turn in the London Eye.

Read on to find the quintessential London Attractions that every tourist should visit.

Trafalgar Square and Nelson's Column

Known as much for its pigeons as for its monuments, Trafalgar Square was opened in 1844 to commemorate the naval battle of Trafalgar, in which the British were victorious, (of course, otherwise why commemorate it?), against France and Spain.

The most famous monument in the Square is Nelson's Column. Admiral Horatio Nelson died at the battle of Trafalgar in 1805. He was, in spite of being dead, considered the victor of the war and his column is known to millions around the world.

Every year since 1947 a Christmas Tree, gifted to Britain from Norway, is erected in the Square. Trafalgar Square is the site of annual New Year's celebrations, and has been the location of major protests against war and climate change.

The tradition of feeding the pigeons seeds was stopped in 2007 as they were considered a health hazard. Something to do with bird flu. The pigeon poop on Nelson's Column caused £140,000 worth of damage!

Buckingham Palace

Of course you must visit the Queen's residence and see the Changing of the Guards. She only occupies a comparatively tiny wing of the imposing palace, which is guarded by soldiers in their characteristic bearskin caps. The Palace has 775 rooms in it! One wonders if she knows her way around it yet?

It also has the largest private garden in London where the Queen hosts her famous Garden Parties every summer. Invitation only for cucumber sandwiches with the crusts trimmed off.

Across the road from Buckingham Palace is the lovely St. James' Park. You can visit the swans, flamingoes and squirrels on your way to the Houses of Parliament and Big Ben. It's probably some of the freshest air you will find in London, so breathe in deep.

Houses Of Parliament

One of the wonderful things about central London is that you actually can walk around it and cover a lot of ground in a short amount of time. Crossing St. James Park really does lead you to the Houses of Parliament and Big Ben, and walking it is absolutely the way to go, if you can. It's a brief 15-minute walk. It gives an airy, magical sense of the sheer majesty of London and it is simply enchanting. Even though you'll need a mask for the fumes once you get out of the park. Remember to pack a few.

The Palace of Westminster is the official title for the Houses of Parliament, as they are more commonly known. The House of Lords meets upstairs and the House of Commons, downstairs. The Palace of Westminster has stood on the spot since the 1100s and was the home of Kings of England until the 1500s when it became Parliament's main hangout. It burned down a few times, including during the Great Fire of London in 1666, and the current construction was designed by the architect James Barry, in the Gothic Revival style, and built between 1840 and 1870.

You can take a tour and even attend debates and committee hearings. What a great way to experience the heart of British politics.

Big Ben

Big Ben is in fact the name of the heaviest of the five bells which is housed in the Elizabeth Tower, at the north end of the Palace. Probably the most iconic symbol of London, and even of the United Kingdom, Big Ben has chimed for the clock and for Londoners for the past 150 years.

From Big Ben it is easy to cross over the Thames at Westminster Bridge and you will find yourself within easy reach of the London Eye and the Thames Embankment.

The London Eye

Also known as the Millennial Wheel, it was built in 1999, just in time for the turning of the century and the millennium. At that time it was the largest Ferris wheel in the world but by now it's only the largest in Europe. It is however the number one most popular, paid for tourist attraction in the UK, so DON'T MISS IT!

It takes about 30 minutes to go round one revolution in one of its capsules, which hold up to 25 people. There is seating but you can stand as well. You walk on and off while the thing is still moving (it goes fairly slowly), although if you are disabled or elderly they stop it for you. Once you get off the London Eye, you will be standing right on the Thames Embankment and it is really fun just to walk along there and see all the street theatre and performers who put on shows there daily. Lots of colourful costumes, jugglers, fire-eaters and statue impersonators.

The Tower Of London

The Tower of London is in reality a whole castle and dates back to the time of the Norman Conquest. That's 1066 we're talking about! It's on the north bank of the River Thames and right next to Tower Bridge, so you can do both these attractions together.

It was originally built as a palace for the new ruling elite (the invaders) but from 1100 until 1952 it was also used as a prison. The infamous Kray brothers were imprisoned there in 1952. Today it houses the Crown Jewels; in fact it has done so since 1662. Another attraction you will see when you visit will be the Beefeaters. Thought to have gotten their name from actually being given large steaks to eat daily, they are formally known as Yeoman Warders. Their job is to guard any prisoner in the tower and to safeguard the crown jewels. Their uniform is the same now as it was in Tudor England!

London Bridge

This particular London Bridge has only been around since 1973, although many more have existed over the centuries. The famous nursery rhyme, "London Bridge is falling down", is singing about this bridge, or its predecessor, to be precise.

It was the only road to cross the River Thames south of Kingston-Upon-Thames, and this was its importance...

Honestly the bridge that is there right now is not the most spectacular thing in the world. BUT you can go to the London Bridge Experience and learn about 2000 years of London's history at its goriest, from Boudicca, British warrior queen and her battle against the Romans, through the Great Fire of London in 1666, to the serial killings of the bloodthirsty Jack the Ripper in Victorian England.

The Shard

Inaugurated in 2012, the Shard is the tallest building in the UK, standing 309.6 metres (1016 feet) high. It is a 95 storey glass tower. Greenpeace protesters have climbed it, Prince Andrew has abseiled down it and others have BASE jumped from it. Urban adventurers have also scaled its dizzying heights. You will most likely take the elevator and sit down to lunch in one of its restaurants admiring the view from the safety of your seating. Or you can go up to the viewing galleries on level 69 and 72, if you really have a head for heights. You can get your souvenirs from the highest store in London, the Sky Boutique, that's level 68. But any reckless undertaking that might ensue as a result of reading this literature is entirely at your own risk.

Piccadilly Circus

Piccadilly Circus has to be at the heart of "just being" in London. A symbol more than the actual centre of London, its famous statue of Eros and illuminated hoardings, coupled with its proximity to Soho, speak of sex, glamour and excitement. Alfred Hitchcock used the setting in no less than five of his films, such was the lure, or the allure, of the lights...Not to burst anyone's bubble or anything but the statue is actually of Anteros, the brother of Eros. Eros stood for romantic love, while Anteros, was mature, selfless love. Take your pick...adilly.

Camden Market

Get your fill of creativity and originality, alongside the second-hand and vintage stalls at Camden Market, a counter-cultural Mecca left over from the seventies, known for its cutting edge music, artsy trend and fashion. Wander by the barges down on Camden lock, and refresh yourself with an ice-cream from Chin Chin Labs, where they use liquid nitrogen to freeze your flavoursome treat right in front of your very eyes.

Best day to visit the market is Sunday, although peak times are weekends. It attracts 100,000 visitors each weekend so expect it to be busy. With over 1000 shops and stalls there is something for everybody.

Chapter 2: Ten Attractions That You Cannot Miss

Covent Garden

One of the prettiest open-air but covered markets you will ever find; Covent Garden is a must-do. Actually the name is of a district from Drury Lane to St Martin's Lane in the West End of London. The Royal Opera House, situated in this district is also known as Covent Garden. There are 13 theatres and 60 pubs and bars, and street performances in daily abundance. This lively and bustling hub will keep you enthralled and entertained for as long as you have time to be there.

Neal's Yard

Neal's Yard is a tiny alley in Covent Garden which opens into a colourful and picturesque courtyard. It houses some quirky cafés, health food stores and the famous blue bottles of Neal's Yard Remedies, home of natural aromatherapy and skin and body care products since 1981. A great photo opportunity here for all the shapes and colours and a souvenir stop for all those eco-minded friends of yours back home.

Shakespeare's Globe Theatre

This is a reconstruction of Shakespeare's playhouse built in the Elizabethan era in 1599. With its thatched roof, timber frame and open-air stage, and a pit where the audience would stand, you can watch live action plays as they would have been seen back in the day. It would have been pretty stinky back then. People didn't wash much and with the gowns worn by the ladies, it was common for them to pee in situ. You want to have an authentic experience but nobody recommends you take it that far...There is some seating on wooden benches available. These are undercover so if it is raining, preferable to the standing area as no umbrellas are allowed. That would spoil the historic atmosphere of the experience. Plays are performed without mics or artificial lighting and music is played on period instruments. The wrought iron gates at the entrance are a fascinating attraction in their own right. Adorned with symbolic motifs wrought by blacksmiths from all over the world, the butterflies, mermaids, spiders, dolphins, whales and bees are allusions to Shakespeare's works. Very cool. So cool in fact you can buy a book just about the gates.

Thames River Boat Cruise

The Thames is the longest river in London and cruising along it by boat is definitely a great way to see the sights of London. You can hop on and off and on again, and rest your legs while you float by any or all of the following:

- Houses of Parliament

- Westminster Abbey

- Big Ben

- The London Eye

- The Tower of London

- Tower Bridge

- Shakespeare's Globe

- Tate Modern

- Cutty Sark

- Canary Wharf

- HMS Belfast battle-cruiser

- Millennium Footbridge

If walking just ain't your thing, you could spend, at least in theory, all your time on a cruise boat. Or you could switch it up and go on one of the London buses, and see things that way too.

London Bus Tour

Sadly, the buses are no longer the classic pillar box red of yore, but they are still double deckers and you can still find ones which are open air on the top deck. You can find ones with tour guides, and ones without tour guides. You can choose various routes which take you past all the great attractions. Again, you can hop on and off as you like at designated stops.

St Paul's Cathedral

An absolute definite if you want to be a fully fledged tourist. This Anglican masterpiece of Baroque architecture was designed by Britain's most famous architect, Sir Christopher Wren, in 1673, after the cathedral was burned to the ground in the Great Fire of London in 1666. That fire burned for four days. A church dedicated to St. Paul has stood on this spot for 1400 years. That's all the way back to 604 AD.

The cathedral is well-known for its magnificent dome and the Whispering Gallery. If you whisper something, another person with their ear to the wall of the Gallery will be able to hear you at any point around the Gallery. It's due to something called "whispering waves" in physics...Pretty cool, huh?

Westminster Abbey

Another jewel in the crown of London, Westminster Abbey is over a thousand years old and is rich in history. It has been the Coronation Church for Kings and Queens of England since 1066, and 17 monarchs are buried there. There have also been 16 royal weddings in the Abbey. William and Kate were married there in 2011 and the current Queen Elizabeth II was crowned on the coronation chair.

Charles Darwin is buried in the grounds along with Charles Dickins and Geoffrey Chaucer.

London Wetland Centre

Situated in a loop of the river Thames, the London Wetland centre is a wonderful way to defuse some of the London fumes and stress, as well as a great family adventure. There is an otter family there and a ton of water birds from around the world including ducks and wading birds. Bats, butterflies and amphibians complete your wetland experience and when you've wandered enough through the marshlands and meadows, you can stop at the café for refreshments. So very English.

London Brass Rubbing Centre

The Church of St. Martin's in the Fields offers a brass rubbing experience. It's a great souvenir and fun for all the family. You take a wax crayon and some sugar paper. Place the paper over one of the brass monuments and decorations on the floor of the church. Rub your crayon over it and you will see an impression of the brass emerge. Today you can choose from over 100 replica brasses to rub. Replicas have been created to avoid damage to the original brasses. But the end result is the same: a stunning work of art to frame and display when you get back home.

Madam Tussauds

The famous wax museum (which includes the London Planetarium) was founded by its namesake in 1835. She had had a touring exhibit up until then of the wax models she inherited from her mentor the Swiss Dr. Curtius. He had taught her the art of wax modelling. One of her original exhibits was the Chamber of Horrors, which showed models of victims of the French Revolution and murderers and other criminals.

Today the museum houses models of politicians, pop stars, movie stars and royalty. The models have real human hair and one gruesome fact is that the model of Adolf Hitler has hair that continuously grows...So creepy!

Chapter 3: Free Entry Museums And Art Galleries

Everybody likes to get something for nothing, don't they? And when you have to pay £3.75 for a cup of coffee in Starbucks in London, you'll be glad to save a few pence here and there. There are some great things to do in London that are absolutely free, so you'd be silly not to take advantage of them. Here are some ideas for you:

The Tate

The Tate Britain, as it is known these days, houses British art from 1500 to the present day.

There are over 4500 artists' works here and you can see styles ranging from the Pre-Raphaelite romanticism of Sir John Everett Millais' Ophelia (1851) to David Hockney's A Bigger Splash (1967). Big names like Picasso, Mark Rothko, Piet Mondrian, Man Ray, Barbara Hepworth, and Kandinsky are just a handful among the thousands of famous artists whose works you can see here. Entrance is free but you pay for the special exhibitions.

The Tate Modern

The Gallery of Modern Art for Britain is housed in a decommissioned power station. Its art starts at Fauvism around 1900 and there are works by Picasso, Matisse, Salvador Dali, Ernst, Miro, Pollock, Giacometti and Rothko. All the major art movements of the modern era are covered and the gallery is internationally renowned. An absolute must for lovers of contemporary art. The gallery has been there since 2000 and, as a head's up, you do have to buy tickets for any temporary exhibitions which are on display. Temporary exhibits have included the work of Indian sculptor Anish Kapoor and controversial Chinese activist artist, Ai Weiwei.

The Victoria And Albert Museum

This is the home of decorative arts and design, dating back to 1852 and housing 4.5 million objects. Collections abound and you can see jewellery, textiles, architecture, ceramics, glass and stained glass, mediaeval tapestries and collections from south Asia, Japan, the Middle East and China. There is so much incredible stuff from all over the world and throughout all the ages that is can get a bit overwhelming. But don't worry. You can take afternoon tea in the café and rest your legs a while. Then you can tick another thing off your "to do" list. The afternoon tea, that is.

The National Gallery

The National Gallery is in Trafalgar Square and it houses 2300 paintings from the 13th to the 20th centuries. Many world famous paintings are housed here by artists such as Van Gogh, Monet, Seurat and Cezanne, Van Eyck, Botticelli, Stubbs, Velazquez and Turner.

Starting in the 13th-15th centuries you can see works by Mantegna, Durer and Bellini. From the 16th century see works by Leonardo, Michelangelo, Holbein, Titian, Veronese and Bruegel. From the 17th century view works by Vermeer, Rembrandt, Caravaggio and Rubens. From the 18th-20th centuries you can see works by Canaletto, Goya, Constable, Ingres, and Degas.

Truly a house of marvels with its priceless works of art from all over the world: you cannot miss this.

The National Portrait Gallery

The National Portrait Gallery opened in1896 and, not surprisingly, it houses portraits of famous people in British history, as well as a few not so famous. 200,000 portraits is a lot, so, it may come as no surprise that you must like portraiture to come here. Portraits date back to the 16th century though, so if you are a history buff then you could probably still enjoy this. The portraits of Henry VIII and Queen Elizabeth I are incredibly informative as to the sumptuousness and the elaborateness of their hand embroidered costumes, as a sign of the wealth, power and prestige that was being displayed.

The British Museum

The British museum is about art, culture and human history. The building alone is worth a visit, with its Roman style. Inside you will find artefacts representing two million years of human history around the world. The oldest artefact is a stone chopping tool from Tanzania, although at first glance it just looks like a lump of rock. But, when you look closely, there is a pattern and uniformity to the blows that caused the rock to have two sides, which narrow down to a sharp edge: perfect for cutting animal flesh or splitting bone to get to the marrow inside. Those blows must have been made by human hands.

The Chinese Jade Room and Egyptian Rooms showing Life, Death and the Afterlife are just some of the many themed galleries you will find. If you have one hour only to visit, or three hours (better) or have children, the museum has splendid ideas for how to make the most of your time there. The three hour highlights itinerary includes the Rosetta Stone, the Holy Thorn Reliquary and the bust of Ramesses. Incredible and priceless treasures from across the globe cannot be given justice in these pages. Just go, and see with your own eyes.

Guildhall Art Gallery

The very first interesting thing about this gallery is that it is sitting smack bang on top of the site of London's Roman amphitheatre. Almost two thousand years ago, up to 7000 viewers sat on benches in the open air to watch the fights between wild animals and gladiators. The circular walls of the amphitheatre were only discovered in 1988 when the site of the new Gallery was being excavated.

The Guildhall Art Gallery was opened in 1886. It houses paintings from 1670 to the present day and includes pre-Raphaelite masterpieces, some portraits from the 17th century and London landscape paintings. Its most famous masterpiece is the Pre-Raphaelite portrait by Dante Gabriel Rosetti, La Ghirlandata (1871-1874).

Southwark Cathedral

Southwark cathedral was a church until 1905, but it dates back to 1106. It was actually a Priory until the dissolution of the monasteries by Henry VIII in 1558. The current Gothic architecture was built between 1220 and 1420 (although the nave is a 19th century reconstruction. But hey, you can't have everything, right?)

It's on the bank of the river Thames and close to London Bridge. There is a really cool 15th century monument to the poet, John Gower. He was Poet Laureate to King Richard II and King Henry IV. The monument really takes you back in time because the original painted colours have been maintained and you see it exactly as it would have looked in mediaeval times. This is pretty unusual and is worth checking out...

Museum Of London

Now this is an amazing museum. It explores the history of the site of London from 450,000 BC to our present times. Did you know London was founded in AD 50? And that 125,000 years ago, the climate and landscape around London were similar to the plains of central Africa as we know them today? Hippos roamed around in what is now Trafalgar Square! Not to mention wolves, rhinos and woolly mammoths! You can learn all about the famous plague and the Great Fire of London in 1666 which destroyed four fifths of the city. On top of the free entry you can take advantage of the free daily guided tour. If you love history you will love the London Museum!

Museum Of London Docklands

Situated in the east of London on the Isle of Dogs, this museum tells the story of the river Thames and the growth of the London docklands. It's not far from Canary Wharf which is worth a visit if you can cram it in. The Docklands Museum is full of original artefacts from the time when the Port of London was a going concern. It gives you a real feel for the hustle and bustle and hard work that went on in the warehouses, as spices, tea and silk were shipped in from China and India.

Imperial War Museum

The Imperial War Museum (IWM) tells the story of war and conflict from World War One to the present time. The IWM is only one third of the equation. There are also:

The Churchill War Rooms

These are set in an actual World War Two bunker and they tell the story of the great man himself, (Sir Winston, that is).

HMS Belfast

This warship displays what life was like onboard at war and at sea from World War Two to 1963.

National Maritime Museum

Since 2012 the Queen approved a new name, Royal Museums Greenwich. Greenwich, where Henry VIII used to live, is to the east of central London and has been a landing port for sea going vessels for centuries. The Royal Museums Greenwich are actually four attractions in one as they include, alongside the National Maritime Museum:

The Royal Observatory Greenwich

The Royal Observatory Greenwich is home to London's only Planetarium where you can relax back in your seat and get your mind blown with the wonders of our solar system, galaxies and the universe. There are a number of shows you can choose from, so whether you want to land on Mars or enter into the heart of the sun, or watch how a star is born, you will feel out of this world, I assure you (groan).

The iconic historic sailing ship Cutty Sark

The Cutty Sark is the world's only surviving tea clipper. She was the fastest ship of her day, in the latter half of the 19th century.

The Queen's House Art Gallery.

The Queen's House was designed 400 years ago by the architect Inigo Jones. It was a gift for Queen Anne of Denmark. She was the wife of King James I. Apparently she accidently killed one of his favourite hunting dogs, during a hunt. He swore at her. She was not happy and, hey presto, he gave her a house. And what a house! It is classical in style, and a break away from the Tudor era. Inigo Jones got the ideas from his travels in

Italy. Very progressive for its day.

In 2016 a wonderful new addition to the Great Hall Ceiling was completed by Turner Prize winning artist Richard Wright. The result is an exquisitely beautiful, ornate design in gold leaf that is simply breath-taking.

And that's not even all...there is still the art gallery and also a ghost. Although there are no guarantees that you will see the ghost.

All Hallows By The Tower

This is the oldest church in the City of London, and dates back to 675.AD. It's next door to the Tower of London and even has a tessellated Roman pavement in its crypt. John Quincy Adams, the sixth President of the United States was actually married there in 1797, and Samuel Pepys watched London burn from this church tower. The founder of Pennsylvania, William Penn, was baptised there in 1644.

Chapter 4: The West End

The West End, London's most prominent commercial and entertainments centre, is deserving of a chapter in its own right. Developed in the 17th-19th centuries as a residential hang-out for the wealthy elite, it was chosen for being down-wind of the London smog and smoke. It is contained mostly within the City of Westminster, one of London's 32 districts or boroughs.

You can differentiate it from the City of London which is the main district for business and finance, and which lies within the Square Mile.

In the era of its development it consisted of expensive homes: palaces and townhouses, fancy stores and theatres, nightclubs, bars and restaurants, and latterly, cinemas.

Although definitions vary as to its boundaries it is said to contain the districts of Mayfair, Soho, Covent Garden, Marylebone and Fitzrovia.

Soho

Soho is renowned for its myriad of theatres, its eating houses and night spots. The Palace theatre, Gielgud Theatre, Lyric Theatre, Queen's Theatre, Palace Theatre, Soho Theatre and London Palladium are all clustered in this one square mile of trend, entertainment and vibrant nightlife.

Famous as the fashionable shopping streets of London's West End, if shopping is your gig, then this is your Mecca.

Oxford Street

A mile and a half long, is best known for its big

department stores and Selfridges, along with many of the well known multinational names. Oxford Street is known as the busiest shopping street in Europe.

Regent Street

Regent Street forms a neat divide between posh Mayfair to the west and trendy Soho to the east. The famous Hamley's toy store is on Regent Street. Otherwise you will find many clothing, shoe and accessory stores with well-known names like Calvin Klein interspersed with lesser known designers like Italy's Stefanel (clothing and accessories) or Japan's Uniqlo (functional and contemporary clothing for all the family).

Bond Street

Bond Street has lots of jewellery stores, accessory stores, art galleries, and leatherwear. "Luxury" is the watch word for this street, and the streets that branch off from it.

Carnaby St

Near Oxford St, Carnaby St is a pedestrianised street well-known for its fashion boutiques and trend. It became popular as a cool fashion destination for both mods and hippies in the Swinging Sixties and a number of famous bands were to be seen there: the mod band Small Faces, The Who and the Rolling Stones... Mary Quant had their designer label there too in the sixties.

Today, hip, trendy and cool are still the words to define this great, colourful collection of designer boutiques and stores, interspersed with fabulous eateries in every proportion you can think of. From Sushi to designer burgers, from purveyors of fine mashed potatoes, to Korean cuisine and American style BBQ, you can find just about any kind of food your heart desires.

West End Theatres

The West End has been home to theatre for hundreds of years, with Drury Lane's Theatre Royal opening in 1663. Today the West End is the largest theatre district in the world, with about 40 venues.

Some of the longest running shows include:

- Agatha Christie's The Mousetrap which has been running non-stop since 1952, currently playing at St. Martin's Theatre

- Les Miserables, running since 1985, currently at the Queen's Theatre

- The Phantom of the Opera, running since 1986 at Her Majesty's Theatre

Shaftesbury Avenue

Shaftesbury Avenue is home to the Lyric, Gielgud, Apollo, Queen's, Palace and Shaftesbury Theatres. It is a wonderfully lively street with an excitable buzz, and many eateries to accompany your show time.

Marble Arch

Designed in 1827 by John Nash, the Marble Arch was originally built to stand in front of Buckingham Palace as the state entrance, but it got moved in 1851 to its current site where it is weirdly isolated. The other weird thing is that the only folks allowed to pass through the arch are the Royal Family and the King's Troop, Royal Horse Artillery; and they do this only during ceremonial processions. But oddity or not, it is a must see as a famous London landmark.

Wallace Collection

In the city of Westminster, the Wallace collection is housed in a historic London townhouse and contains many fine French 18th century paintings, Old Masters and a collection of armour, too. Furniture and porcelain are on display, and it's another museum with free admission.

L. Ron Hubbard's Fitzroy House

L. Ron Hubbard holds the Guinness World Record for most published author (1084 works) and is the founder of Scientology. His house, dating back to 1791, is in the heart of Fitzrovia. Fitzrovia was home to numerous artists and writers, including Charles Dickens, Virginia Wolf, H.G. Wells and George Orwell. George Bernard Shaw lived for a short time on the very same house that L. Ron Hubbard resided in. Visits are by appointment only, but you will find a museum dedicated to the life and work of Mr. Hubbard.

Sherlock Holmes' Residence

221b Baker Street is the address of the famous fictional detective. The townhouse dating back to 1815, between numbers 237 and 241 Baker Street, is now home to a museum in his name. The museum is set up as a representation of the rooms Sherlock and Dr. Watson would have resided in during the years 1881-1904. It is like stepping back through time but also into a slightly alternative reality; the rooms are put together using all authentic pieces from the era, and the atmosphere and mood is quite convincing.

Regent's Park

If you are looking for a bit of decompression then by now it will be time for a visit to Regent's Park, one of London's Royal Parks. Lakes, fountains, an amphitheatre, cafes, rose garden and even a cricket pitch await you. There is a children's playground and you can feed the ducks, then wander up the beautiful Primrose Hill for a fabulous view of the city at sunset.

London Zoo

London Zoo is right in the middle of Regent's Park, so it makes sense to visit them together... London Zoo has been open since 1828 and it is the world's oldest "scientific" zoo. It was supposed to be for scientific study. With 755 species of animals, an aquarium, a reptile house and even a spider house, you will not be bored. Whether you like bugs, bats, butterflies and birds, or lemurs, lions and leopards, or giraffes, gorillas and Galapagos tortoises, or penguins and pigmy hippos, London Zoo is the largest collection in the UK. Be prepared to walk a lot, bring plenty of bottled water and comfy shoes. You'll have a great day out.

Leicester Square

Leicester Square dates back to 1670 and is surrounded by cinemas, restaurants and more theatres. It had a complete makeover to the tune of £17 million in time for the 2012 Olympics. You can get good deals on tickets to west end theatre performances here at the TKTS booth. There is a statue of Shakespeare, grassy lawns and fountains. Street theatre happens daily, there is a Christmas market held here and Chinese New Year celebrations too. And don't forget to visit the Lego Store...

Burlington Arcade

The Burlington Arcade is a covered shopping

arcade in Mayfair. Opened in 1819 it now has about 40 stores under a glass roof. It is very upmarket, and antique silverware, jewellery and art are among its attractions. It is worth going to see the "beadles" who patrol the arcade. They wear top hats and frock coats to this day.

Chapter 5: Haunted London

With so much history and so many centuries behind it, you won't be surprised to learn that London is reputedly the most haunted capital city in the world. And who doesn't like a good ghost story, especially when it's a true one? So here are some of the best haunts around London.

The Ten Bells Pub

The Ten Bells was the local pub of Jack the Ripper, a famous, or more appropriately, infamous, serial killer who roamed the streets of Victorian London in the dead of night, when he would encounter his unfortunate female victims. The Ten Bells pub houses a number of ghosts, although not one of them was killed by the Ripper himself, according to belief. One of these ghouls is an old man dressed in Victorian clothing. It is believed to be the ghost of one of the Publicans of the Ten Bells, who was murdered with an axe in a Swansea pub. What he was doing down in Swansea is anybody's guess. It seems that brutal and cold blooded murder was quite popular back then. If you take a room there, in the Ten Bells, you might roll over to find the old man lying in the bed next to you. Ewww...

Jack The Ripper Tour

Not exactly ghostly material but utterly grisly and gruesome nonetheless, you can go on a tour of Jack the Ripper's stomping grounds in the poverty-stricken, overcrowded Whitechapel area of the East End of London in 1888. The true identity of the serial killer was never discovered. He targeted female prostitutes, killed them by slitting their throats and then disembowelled them or removed parts of their intestinal anatomy. The murderer killed anywhere between five and eleven women over a period of three years, although it is not conclusive as to how many of these murders were the work of a single person. At least five follow the same MO.

Handel's House Museum

Handel lived in this house in Mayfair from 1723 until his death in 1759. However the non-malevolent spirit that has been viewed there by several people, seems to be of the female persuasion. It is speculated that it may be the ghost of one of two female visitors, sopranos who wanted to be in Handel's operas.

The Charterhouse

Ghosts or no ghosts, this is London's only surviving Tudor townhouse and deserving of a visit for its historical value and interest. Situated on the site of a 14th century monastery, victims of the Black Death lie buried beneath the square in front of the house. It is said that the ghost of a monk haunts the premises. Many monks were brutally executed here by Henry VIII before the monastery's final dissolution, so no wonder really that at least one of the monks is still floating around.

After this the building became a private residence and Elizabeth I was entertained here on two occasions. Thomas Howard, 4th Duke of Norfolk, then bought the house. He wanted to marry Mary Queen of Scots, and this led to him being arrested on the stairs of the house; he was later executed. The Ghost of the Duke of Norfolk is said to walk down that very same staircase with his head tucked neatly under his arm. He certainly knows how to haunt with style!

Sutton House

Sutton House in East London was built of red brick in 1535 by Sir Ralph Sadleir, one of Henry VIII's Privy Councillors. Its oak panelled walls and great staircase are the perfect Tudor backdrop for a ghostly encounter. The dogs of John Machell, a rich wool merchant who lived in the house between 1550 and 1558 are sometimes heard howling and wailing. When dogs enter the house they stare at the staircase with their hackles raised, as if seeing something that we humans cannot. The ghost of the White Lady also inhabits Sutton House. She is said to be the ghost of the wife of John Machell the Younger. She died giving birth to twins in 1574. She wears a blue dress and glides around the building.

Other ghostly goings-on in Sutton House include sudden drops in temperature, doors opening by themselves and objects flying across the room. Spooky indeed. Visit if you dare...

Chapter 6: Nightlife

Of course the nightlife in London is endless and the choices overwhelming. Pubs, bars and nightclubs abound. Pubs are the quintessentially great British tradition, whilst London has some of the greatest nightclubs, well, ever. Here is just a tiny selection of some of the best...

Fabric

London's leading club, opposite Smithfield meat market. Maybe not a coincidence? Fabric has three massive dance floors and is inside a converted cold store...Drum, bass and dubstep nevertheless on Friday night, with house, techno and electronica on Saturday. You have to get your tix in advance because it is so popular.

Cargo

Close enough to the Jersualem Tavern, in Clerkenwell, Shoreditch and Spitalfields, this is London's most eclectic club. Check it out if only for the original Bansky artworks on the walls outside. You'll hear hip hop, R&B, pop and club classics underneath the brick railway arches where the dance floor is found.

Ministry Of Sound

This club in Greenwich, south London, offers trance on Fridays and house, techno and electro on Saturdays. With four bars, three dance floors and top DJs, Ministry of Sound continues to hold its own among the top ranking clubs in London.

Corsica Studios

Two rooms of music and a bar in this award-winning south London venue is popular with students and offers dubstep, garage and experimental sounds.

Jerusalem Tavern In Clerkenwell, Shoreditch and Spitalfields

Very popular and highly atmospheric pub dating back to 1720, this pub will serve you amazing beer from the St Peter's brewery in Suffolk. It does get busy though.

Lamb And Flag

If jazz is your preference the West End Lamb and Flag pub hosts jazz nights on the first Sunday of every month. If you can't make it to the jazz night you will want to visit for its antiquated charm and buzz. The pub dates back to 1772 and used to be known as the Buckets of Blood, for all the fighting that went on there. A cheerier and more peaceable crowd now frequents its rooms, and you can admire the old fashioned brass fittings as you force your way through the hoards to order your drink at the bar. If you can manage to catch the attention of the barman, you'll be lucky.

The Harp

In central London's Chandos Place, The Harp is a very "pubby" pub, with decorations consisting of a collection of beer mats. Great beers, real ale, cider and sausages.

POLPO: Ape And Bird

A gastropub in Covent Garden serving Venetian-style small plates and wood-fired pizza.

Bar Soho

Central, a somewhat Sherlock Holmesesque interior, quirky cocktail bar, and goes from chill to party with DJs every night.

Quaglino's

In the West End, an opulent and decadent experience with art deco bar and modernist lighting. Fantastically original European and Middle Eastern cuisine, great liquor and live music and DJs and late nights on the weekends.

Chapter 7: Eating Out

Alongside the great British traditions of bangers and mash, and fish and chips, you will find food from every ethnicity in the world to tantalise your taste buds. There is so much choice, and cafes, bars, pubs and restaurants are ubiquitous. So to help you find fine dining, here is a taste of some of the best and most popular restaurants you will find in London, whether you are looking for gourmet or budget dining.

Alain Ducasse at The Dorchester Hotel (14th) in Mayfair

Chef Ducasse is one of France's top chefs. This restaurant has three Michelin stars (that's a lot) and is known for serving fabulously original dishes such as a lobster with truffled chicken starter.

Restaurant Gordon Ramsay

Another restaurant with three Michelin stars to its name, Gordon Ramsay's Chelsea restaurant is one of the top places to eat in London. He makes food into art.

La Gavroche

If you want to eat frog's legs in London then this is the place for you. Classic French, La Gavroche in Mayfair is Chef Michel Roux Jr.'s creation and has two Michelin stars.

The Greenhouse

The Greenhouse in Mayfair is a two Michelin starred restaurant with a unique menu and stunning desserts. Fancy the Chestnut with Yuzu and Honey and Guinness Ice Cream?

Golden Hind

This has to be your classic British experience. The Golden Hind has been serving fish and chips since 1914. And if you're on a budget the price won't give you a heart attack; but that deep fried batter just might. In Farringdon.

Hoppers

Very highly appraised Sri Lankan and south Indian cuisine on Frith Street. Hoppers are a kind of pancake and dosas are a kind of lentil pancake...

Brasserie Zedel

Parisian style at rock-bottom prices in Picadilly Circus.

Berber And Q Shawarma Bar

Based in Clerkenwell, Middle Eastern kebabs, lamb kofte, lamb shawarma, pita, tahini, pickles and herbs. Are you salivating yet?

The Good Life Eatery

This is for the health conscious foodies among you. Smoothies, juices, bee pollen and fresh, feisty salads and vegetable dishes predominate, although fish and meat are also served. Based in Chelsea.

Bao

Bao in Soho is renowned for serving London's best buns. Their signature bun is pork belly, peanut powder and pickled lettuce. Oh, and the price is right.

Bibimbap

Also in Soho, this Korean restaurant serves you its namesake, a layered dish of rice, spiced vegetables, meat and fried egg.

Butifarra

It's in Chinatown but the menu is South

American. A Peruvian style selection includes sandwiches and sweet arepas(a kind of cooked cornmeal patty).

Chapter 8: Things To Do With Kids

If you are bringing your family with you and you have young children, then you need this section. There is nothing worse than having a whiney kid in tow, dragging them around an exhibit that is dry, dull and plain boring. When history and science come alive then they can be fascinating, and more and more museums are onboard with this nowadays. You will find activity trails and interactive features in many of them, which helps make the experience for your children, and therefore for you, so much happier!

V & A For Kids

The leading museum for art and design in

London encourages families to visit with their children and to entice you they offer free activities daily. There is a state-of-the-art digital studio where kids can try their hands at 3D printing or design their own beautiful patterns for their fashion designs. There is green screen photography too. Aside from the tech world there are puzzles and games to do as you tour round the museum or hands on arts and crafts activities.

The Arcelor Mittal Orbit

This landmark was built to commemorate the 2012 Olympic and Paralympic Games and is constructed of steel by the steel company, Arcelor Mittal. The wonderful thing about this tower is that there is a huge, transparent, tubular slide inside the steel structure, which makes for a hair-raising adventure! Once you've taken the elevators up to the top and admired the panoramic view of London, you can either go back down the way you came up, or take the 455 stairs, if you are really energetic. But if you want a hair-raising adventure you can take the fast way down: a 40 second ride through a looping and corkscrewing tubular slide which at times lets you see the London landscape and at times sends you into darkness! Not for the faint of heart but something you will definitely remember forever!

The site was re-opened in 2014 as the Queen Elizabeth Olympic Park and it is now home to wetlands, meadows and waterways.

Little Angel Puppet Theatre

Situated in Islington, the Little Angel Puppet Theatre is London's only permanent puppet theatre. It has been showing puppet theatre since 1961. Geared up for kids, there is a Puppet Club every Saturday. The puppets are carved and created on site and there are participatory workshops and events available. The shows are aimed at audiences from the very, very young (18 months), all the way to teen (14) and adult audiences. Very much a family affair.

China Town

Situated in London's West End, China Town is such a fun thing to do for all the family and if you are lucky enough to be there during the Chinese New Year you will have a blast! One of the great attractions of China Town of course is the authentic Chinese cuisine you will encounter and the numerous restaurants to choose from. The bustle and excitement of this part of London will sweep you up in its cheer, as you pass signs in both English and Mandarin, sculptures of dragons and colourful lanterns, gift stores and food stores galore.

London Dungeon

This is a great attraction for families with kids of age 12 or older, as it can be a wee bit scary for the younger ones. Twenty different shows with 360 degree sets show a thousand years of London's history in a thrilling, humourous and exciting style. While having fun, shivers and shrieking with laughter at one moment and terror the next, you will learn fascinating facts about Guy Fawkes who tried to blow up the houses of Parliament, the London Plague, the Great Fire, the world of Henry VIII, the barbaric barber Sweeney Todd, and the vicious murderer Jack the Ripper. With authentic audio visual effects all around you and great actors to draw you back in time, you will really experience what life was like in historic London. Even the smells will convince you: like the smells of rat poop and pee for example...not for the squeamish this exhibit.

Harry Potter: Warner Brothers Studio Tour and Transfers

This tour will require a day but you board the bus in central London and get taken to the studios, where you have about 4 hours to look around. You get to walk on the actual sets where the Harry Potter movie was filmed and you can even walk along Diagon Alley. Plus you can go for a ride on the Hogwarts Express, leaving from Platform 9 ¾ of course. You can try drinking butterbeer and practise your broomstick riding skills!

Kidzania London

This attraction only opened in 2015 and is the first kid-centred educational entertainments exhibit in the UK. In a child-sized world, children are encouraged to try out different careers. What is it like to be a pilot? An actor or a tour guide? A firefighter or a film camera operator? The kid friendly city covers 75,000 square feet. Children can explore while they learn. It is suitable for children from age 4-14.

Shrek's Adventure

For 6-13 year olds, but lots of fun for the grown-up kids in the family too! This is London's newest attraction. It just opened in 2015 and you get to star in your own family adventure with the inimitable Donkey as your guide. Lots of fun and laughter as you meet the characters from the movie, including the Princess Fiona, Puss in Boots, Gingy the Gingerbread man and the Three Little Pigs. You start out in a red London bus with Donkey showing you the sites! You cruise through

10 fairy-tale shows and you have to find all the magical ingredients to make sure you can get back home. You will meet a few scary witch characters so only the bravest of the brave should go to this.

Legoland Windsor

Legoland Windsor makes a great day out for a family with children ages 3-12. There are over 55 rides and attractions and a great pirate show with real pirates and real water! The Land of the Vikings ride was fun and lots of water there too! You get wet. But don't worry they have these awesome dryers you can actually climb into and get a blow dry for your whole body! Be sure to try out the JCR diggers. Real diggers to work and play around on. If you've never done it before it requires some skill; harder for the grown-ups to master, of course. Fire Academy is quite good too with the whole family working together as a team to put out the flames on a burning building. (The flames are not real ones, of course!). Hmmm, however it does involve water again. Best to go on a sunny day to this one...There are other ways to get drenched here too! Lots to do and who didn't love Lego as a child?

Ripley's Believe It Or Not

This is a good exhibition for families with kids of all ages. American Robert Ripley lived from 1890-1949 and he travelled the world in search of the weird and the wonderful. In Ripley's Believe It Or Not London, you will see a model of London Bridge made entirely of matchsticks and a portrait of Kate Middleton made of lipstick kisses and canvas. You will see some of Ripley's original collection including shrunken human heads from the Amazon. There is a display of beauty as perceived by different cultures. Ripley celebrated the diverse curiosity of humanity and one of his great friends was 8 feet 11 inches tall: the tallest man who ever lived. The exhibit displays the lives of other curious humans: the man who underwent body modifications to look like a lizard; the man who lost his nose in a swordfight and replaced it with one made of solid gold; the man with double pupils in his eyes! And that's just for starters! Over

700 artefacts and exhibits are housed here, from the kitsch to the bizarre.

Chapter 9: Top Things to Do In London That Other Tourists Don't Know About

There is so much to do in London but here are top fascinating gems that even most Londoners won't know about. You can consider yourselves "in the know".

Chelsea Physic Garden

A charming walled garden beside the Thames, this is London's earliest botanical garden, established in 1673. It contains 5000 species of medicinal and historic plants.

The Rolling Bridge, Paddington Basin.

This bridge was designed by its creator, Thomas Heatherwick, to roll up into an octagon shape every Friday at noon! Definitely worth a butcher's, as they say in Cockney (East London) rhyming slang (butcher's hook = look).

The Seven Noses of Soho.

Designed in 1997 by artist Rick Buckley, he supposedly hung 35 noses but only seven remain. Urban myth states that the one in Admiralty Arch was erected to mock Napoleon. It is said that if you find all seven you will be wealthy for evermore...

The Hidden Ears of Covent Garden

Artist Tim Fishlock installed two sculpted ears on Floral Street. More are purportedly hidden around. How many will you find?

The Whitechapel Bell Foundry

Big Ben and the Liberty bell were both forged here and it is a working foundry to this day.

The Victorian Pet Cemetery In Hyde Park.

You can't go in but you can look through the bars and read the inscriptions. Very sentimental and very Victorian. It's in the north-west section of Hyde Park by Victoria Gate Lodge.

Britain's Smallest Police Station

You can find it on the east side of Trafalgar Square. It was built in the 1800s and was used for police to stand in during protests and riots, and keep a lookout. It's only used for storage today. The lamp on top came from Nelson's ship, HMS Victory, or so they say...

The Freud Museum

Yes...You too can visit the famous couch that's

Freud's patients were treated upon. But don't get caught lying down on it, OK? Freud emigrated to London to flee the Nazis in 1938 and the museum shows where he lived and his collection of antiquities.

William Morris Gallery

An ode to the Arts and Crafts master himself, this gallery, to be found in Walthamstow, is the house Morris grew up in. Its exhibits include the sumptuous fabrics, wallpapers and furniture that are the epitomy of the Morris style.

Old Operating Theatre Museum

Now this one is funky, freaky and authentic. As if designed to creep you out, you will climb a winding and rickety staircase to the creaky attic in the top of a Southwark church. This attic was purposely built to be an operating theatre, which in itself is strange since it is at the top of a church. It makes you wonder, doesn't it? It is the oldest operating theatre in the UK and is equipped with original instruments and artefacts. In the 19th century they used things like hacksaws and alcohol...

Little Venice

London's answer to Italy's gem. In fact it is nothing like the city of romance and masquerades, but it is quaint and fairy-tale in its own sweet way. Canal boats and barges jostle end-to-end and pubs, restaurants and cafes line the way. On your way to Camden or Regent's Park, this hidden gem will delight you.

Final words

So there you have it. Your trip to London all laid out for you and ready to go. Rest assured that this book gives you 101 of the best attractions and things that you must do in London that you can find.

Depending on your time limitations, you will need to pick and choose. Of course you will have to do the essentials, the very top tourist attractions. But then you get to decide on the quirkier and more unusual places to visit.

But seriously, with a great list like this, you cannot go far wrong. Have a wonderful trip and remember to do the right British thing, and send home a postcard to the folks back home, saying,

"Wish you were here"!

Bonus: the Secret for Cheap Flights

Did you know there are travelers who never pay for flights? Or when they pay, they pay very little.

Some are people who travel full time. Some are people with normal jobs. Some are moms and dads, others are single travelers.

They're the same as everyone else - with **one big exception:**

They don't pay for flights. They can travel anywhere they want, whenever they want.

So before you travel, make sure you know the 3 tips to get the cheapest flights possible.

There are 3 ways you can get cheap flights.

1) Use Error Fares

2) Use Throwaway Tickets

3) Get (Almost) Free Flights

1. Look for Error Fares

Error fares are cheap plane tickets that the airlines put up online by mistake. You can find these on websites like SecretFlying.com or AirfareWatchdog.com.

These flights can be as much as 50% below what you'd normally pay. That said, they only leave from certain destinations and only go to certain places.

2. Use Throwaway Tickets

Did you know it's sometimes cheaper to book a LONGER flight.. and throw away the second portion?

Example: Instead of booking New York to Texas, it might be cheaper to book a ticket from New York to Los Angeles, with a layover in Texas.

Just get off at the layover and discard the 2nd leg of the flight.

3. The Secret to book $1,000 flights for just $20 or less. (MOST IMPORANT)

This strategy is the easiest and most effective of the three. By using a few tricks to earn frequent flyer miles really quickly (without being a frequent flyer,) you can basically get free flights over and over and over.

As a small token of my appreciation for you reading this book, I have a FREE gift for you showing this **Secret to book $1,000 flights for just**

$20 or less.

Check out the video showing you how on my website at: www.JamesHallTravel.com/TravelHack

I hope that it would help you save money on your flight tickets like I did, so you can travel more and enjoy what life has to offer!

Enjoy!

James Hall

Thanks for reading! If you like the book, please write a short review on Amazon with your thoughts. Also, if you like this book, please let others know, in order to share the awesomeness of London!

Check out my other books...

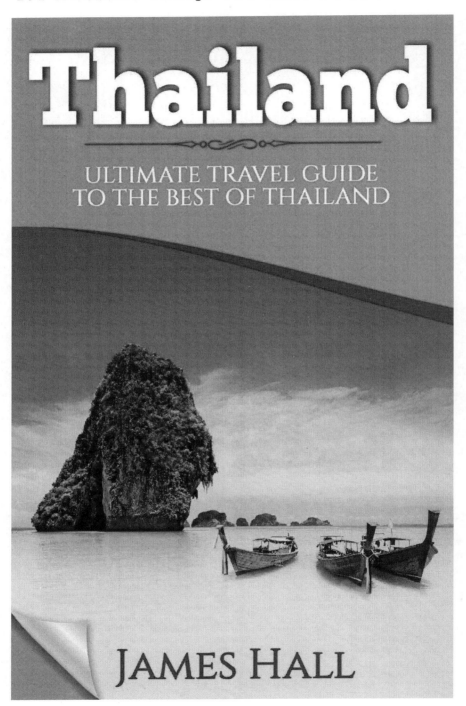

Thailand

ULTIMATE TRAVEL GUIDE TO THE BEST OF THAILAND

JAMES HALL

Still interested in my other travel books?

I have many more to come. I intend to write about all the places that I traveled to.

Connect with me on my website at www.JamesHallTravel.com, or check out my Amazon Author Page for my new books: https://www.amazon.com/James-Hall/e/B01M5K2N8F.

Made in the USA
Lexington, KY
30 June 2017